IT'S ELECTRIC!
CURRENTS

Carla Mooney

Rourke
Educational Media

rourkeeducationalmedia.com

Before Reading:

Building Academic Vocabulary and Background Knowledge

Before reading a book, it is important to tap into what your child or students already know about the topic. This will help them develop their vocabulary, increase their reading comprehension, and make connections across the curriculum.

1. *Look at the cover of the book. What will this book be about?*
2. *What do you already know about the topic?*
3. *Let's study the Table of Contents. What will you learn about in the book's chapters?*
4. *What would you like to learn about this topic? Do you think you might learn about it from this book? Why or why not?*
5. *Use a reading journal to write about your knowledge of this topic. Record what you already know about the topic and what you hope to learn about the topic.*
6. *Read the book.*
7. *In your reading journal, record what you learned about the topic and your response to the book.*
8. *After reading the book complete the activities below.*

Content Area Vocabulary
Read the list. What do these words mean?
alternating current
ampere
atom
circuit
conductor
direct current
discharge
electric current
electron
force
generator
insulators
load
parallel circuit
power plant
resistance
series circuit
turbine
volt
watt

After Reading:

Comprehension and Extension Activity

After reading the book, work on the following questions with your child or students in order to check their level of reading comprehension and content mastery.

1. *How are atoms and matter connected? (Asking questions)*
2. *What are some ways you use direct currents (DC) and alternating currents (AC)? (Text to self connection)*
3. *Explain the different ways electricity can be generated. (Summarize)*
4. *Why is plastic used in electrical cords, light switches, extension cords, and Christmas lights? (Infer)*
5. *How is electricity measured? (Summarize)*

Extension Activity

Opposites attract! As we read in the book, positive and negative electrons are attracted to each other. Using a blown up balloon and water from your faucet you will be able to see this attraction in action. First, turn on the faucet so that the water flows out in a small but steady stream. Next, charge the balloon by rubbing it over dry hair several times. Now, slowly bring the balloon near the water. What happens? Why did this happen?

TABLE OF CONTENTS

CHAPTER ONE

WHAT IS ELECTRICITY?

Every day, you depend on electricity. At home, your refrigerator, television, and telephones use electricity. In factories, machines operate with electricity. At businesses, elevators and cash registers run using electricity.

Electricity that powers the world travels as an **electric current**. An electric current is created by the flow of electrical charges. To understand how this happens, you need to first step inside the world of atoms.

Atoms are the building blocks that make up matter. Matter is anything that has mass and takes up space. Tiny atoms form all matter. They are so small that millions of atoms would fit on the head of a pin.

Individual atoms have even smaller particles called protons, electrons, and neutrons. An atom's protons and neutrons are found in its center, the nucleus. Electrons orbit the nucleus, like the planets around the Sun.

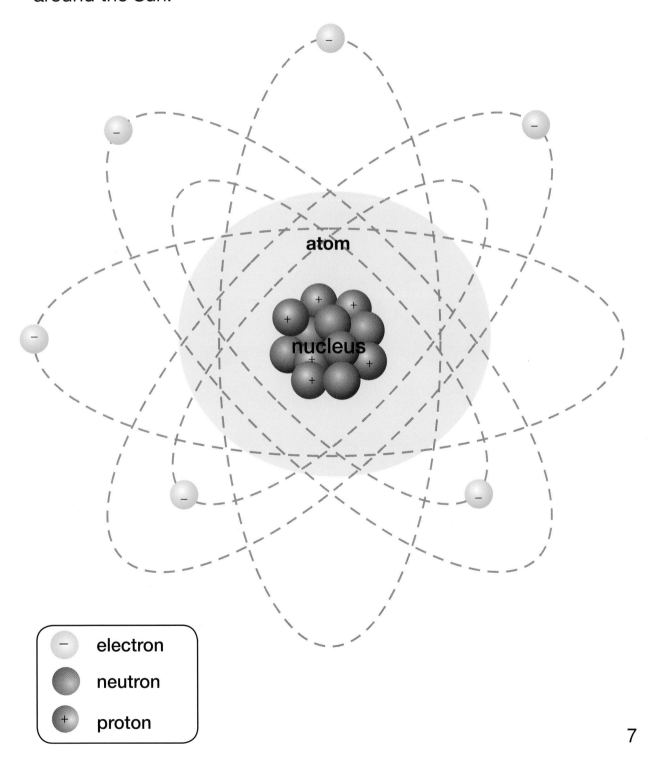

electron

neutron

proton

Protons and electrons have an electrical charge. Protons have a positive charge (+), while electrons have a negative charge (-). Opposite charges attract each other, like magnets. Therefore, protons (+) attract electrons (-).

At the same time, like charges repel each other. Protons repel protons, while electrons repel electrons.

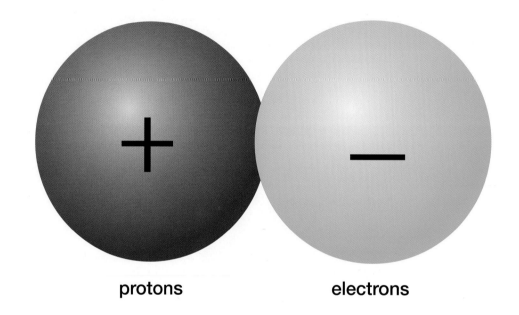

protons   electrons

Protons attract electrons due to their opposite charge.

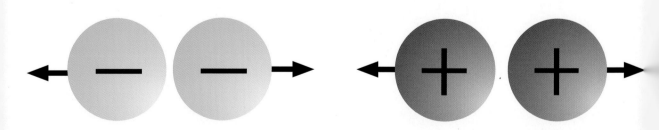

Because of their like charge, electrons repel electrons and protons repel protons.

Atoms start with an equal number of protons and electrons. The protons' positive charges offset the electrons' negative charges. The atom's charge is neutral.

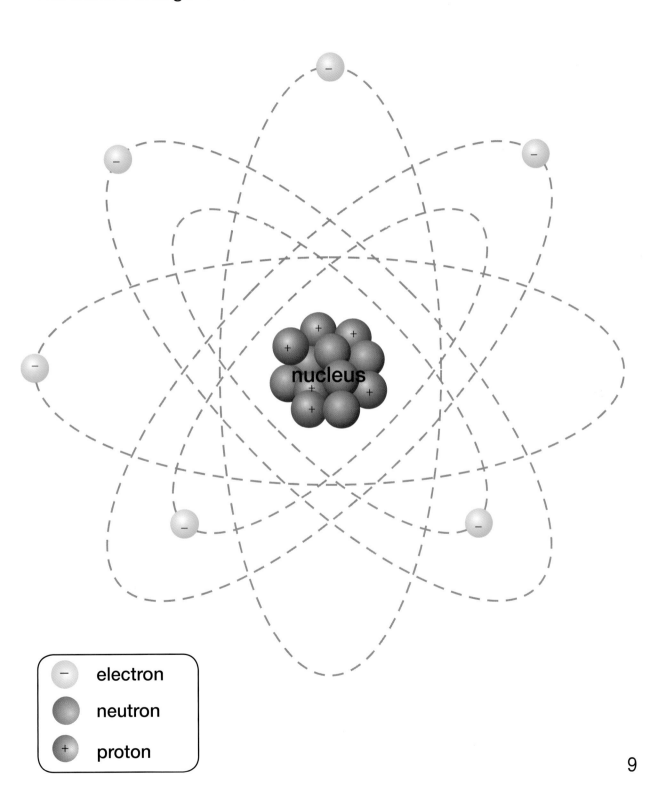

−	electron
●	neutron
+	proton

Sometimes, electrons move from **atom** to atom. Friction is one way that objects gain or lose electrons. When an **electron** moves to a new atom, that atom now has more electrons than protons, giving it a negative charge. The negative electrons repel each other, causing another electron to move to another atom. The flow of electrons creates an electric current.

Electric current is the flow of the electric charge.

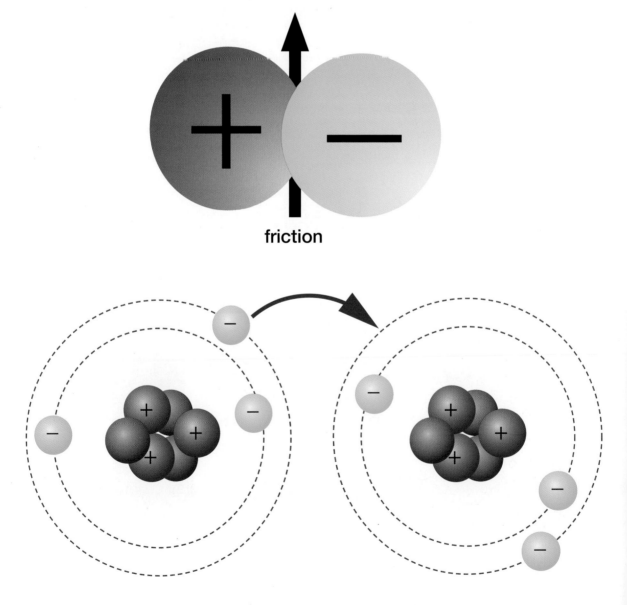

friction

Electric Current

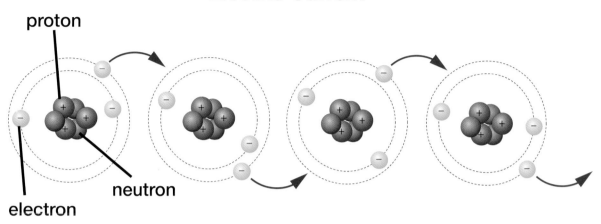

proton

neutron

electron

Electric current is generated when electrons move from atom to atom.

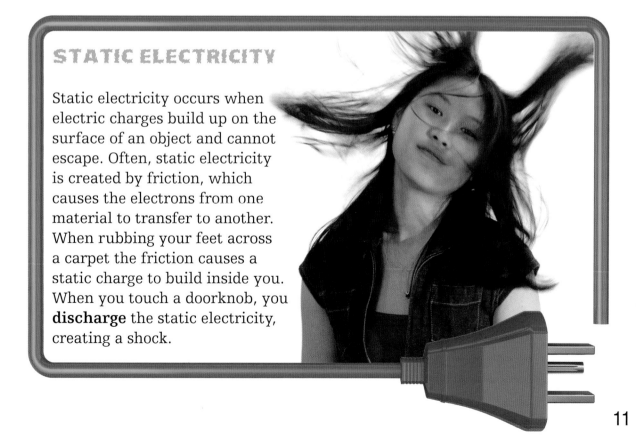

STATIC ELECTRICITY

Static electricity occurs when electric charges build up on the surface of an object and cannot escape. Often, static electricity is created by friction, which causes the electrons from one material to transfer to another. When rubbing your feet across a carpet the friction causes a static charge to build inside you. When you touch a doorknob, you **discharge** the static electricity, creating a shock.

Electric current flows through some materials more easily than others. Materials that let electrons move freely are called conductors. Conductors have atoms that lose electrons easily.

The most conductive material is silver. Because silver is rare and expensive, most electrical wiring and circuits use copper as a conductor instead.

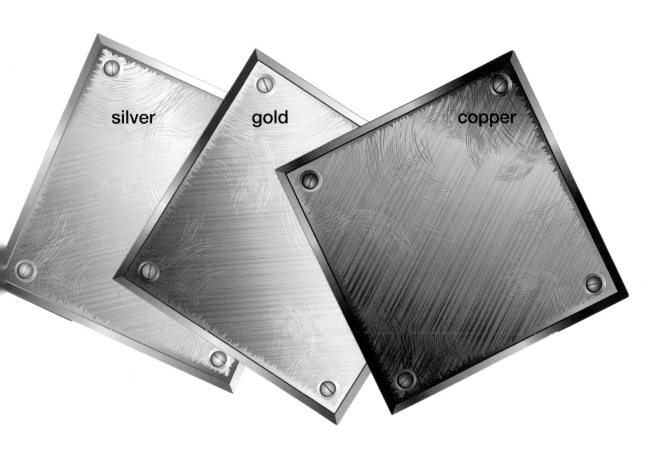

silver

gold

copper

Metals are an example of an electrical **conductor**. Copper, silver, and gold are some of the best metal conductors. Some gases, such as neon, can also conduct electricity. Liquids, such as mercury and salt water, are also good conductors.

neon

Other substances called **insulators** resist the flow of electric current. Plastic, rubber, cloth, and glass are examples of insulators. These materials hold electrons tightly. Insulators are often used to protect you from electricity.

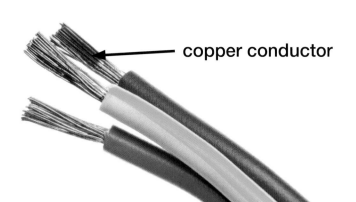

copper conductor

rubber insulator

Power cords have a rubber coating that keeps the electric current inside. Light switches are covered in plastic to prevent you from getting a shock when you turn on the lights.

ELECTRIC SAFETY

While you use electricity every day, it is important to remember that it can be dangerous. Keep these important safety rules in mind:

1. Electricity is not a toy. Never play with electricity.
2. Follow the directions on electrical equipment. Ask an adult for help.
3. Do not pull a cord from an outlet, remove the plug carefully. Pulling the cord can damage the outlet, the plug, or the appliance.
4. Never stick anything into an electrical outlet except an approved plug.
5. Never use electronic items near water.
6. Do not overload an outlet or an extension cord.
7. Have an adult put safety caps in any unused electrical outlets.

CHAPTER TWO

ELECTRIC CIRCUITS

How does electric current reach the device it powers? It travels on an electric **circuit**!

Electrons flow only when they have somewhere to go. An electric circuit is the complete path on which electric current flows. It begins in one place, travels around the circuit, and returns to its starting place.

A simple electric circuit has three parts: a power source, a **load**, and a conducting wire that connects them.

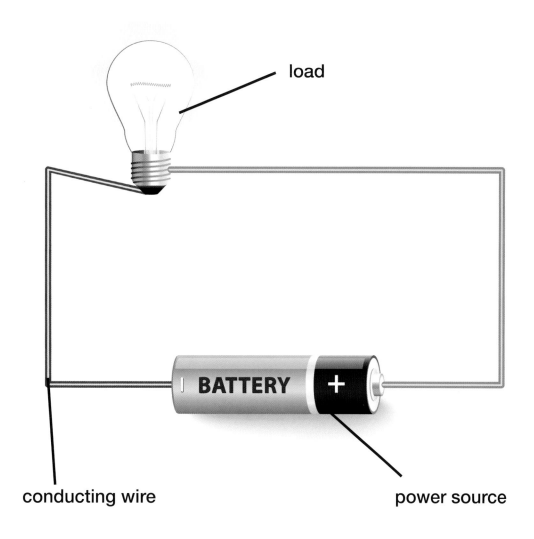

load

conducting wire

power source

Circuits can be very complex. They can have thousands of components.

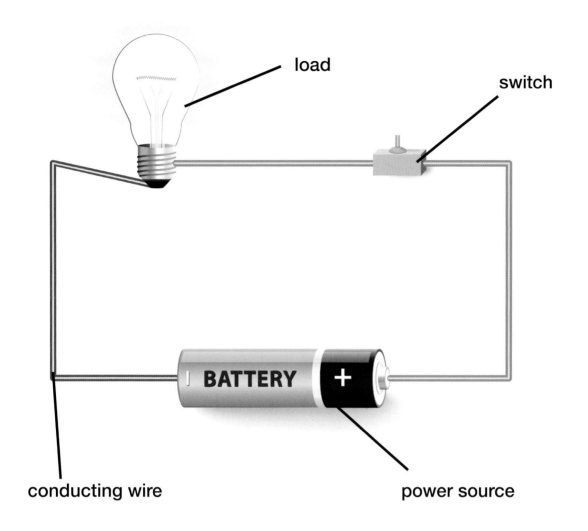

load

switch

conducting wire

power source

BATTERY +

One common way to control an electric current is with a switch. A closed switch connects the circuit, allowing electric current to flow. An open switch disconnects the circuit, creating a gap that the current cannot cross.

When electric current flows through a circuit, it generates heat. Too much heat can melt the insulation of electrical wires and start a fire. Fuses and circuit breakers sense the heat in the circuit. If too much heat builds, they break the circuit to stop the flow of electric current.

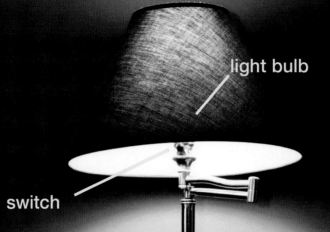

light bulb

switch

In a simple circuit that carries electric current to a lamp, electric current flows from a power source. It moves through metal conducting wires. When the lamp's switch is turned on, the electric circuit is complete and closed. The light turns on. If the switch is turned off, there is a gap in the circuit that the electric current cannot cross. The light does not turn on.

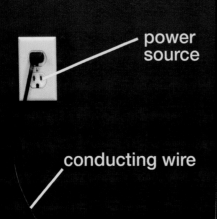

power source

conducting wire

SCHEMATIC DIAGRAMS

Electric circuits are often described using a schematic diagram. The diagram shows how the components of a circuit connect. Electricians use standard symbols when drawing a schematic diagram of a circuit.

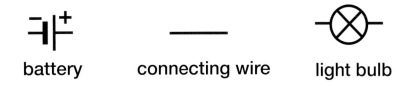

battery   connecting wire   light bulb

switch (open)   switch (closed)

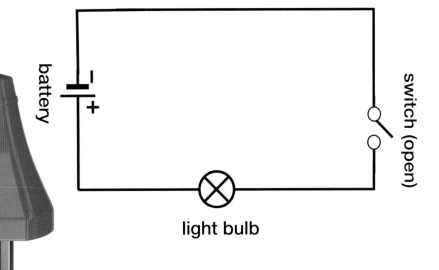

Some electrical circuits are series circuits. Like a one-way street, series circuits have only one way for the electric current to flow. There may be several loads and switches along the circuit. If the circuit is broken in any place, the current stops. None of the loads receives power.

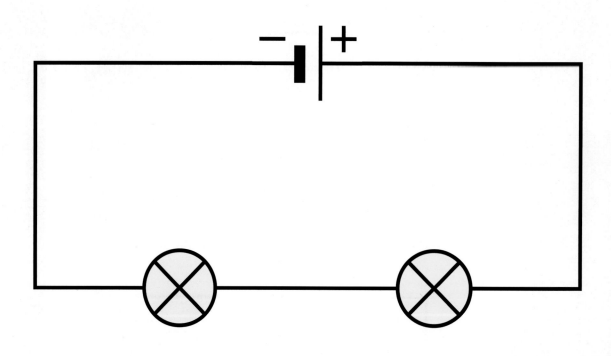

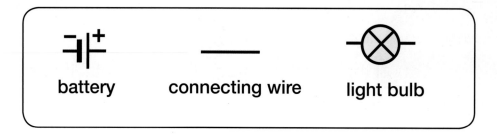

| battery | connecting wire | light bulb |

Some holiday lights work in a **series circuit**. The current flows one way through the string, lighting all of the lights. If one light is removed, the closed loop is broken. No current flows and the entire string goes dark.

Parallel circuits allow current to flow along more than one path. If a **parallel circuit** has a break, the current can still travel through the circuit using another route.

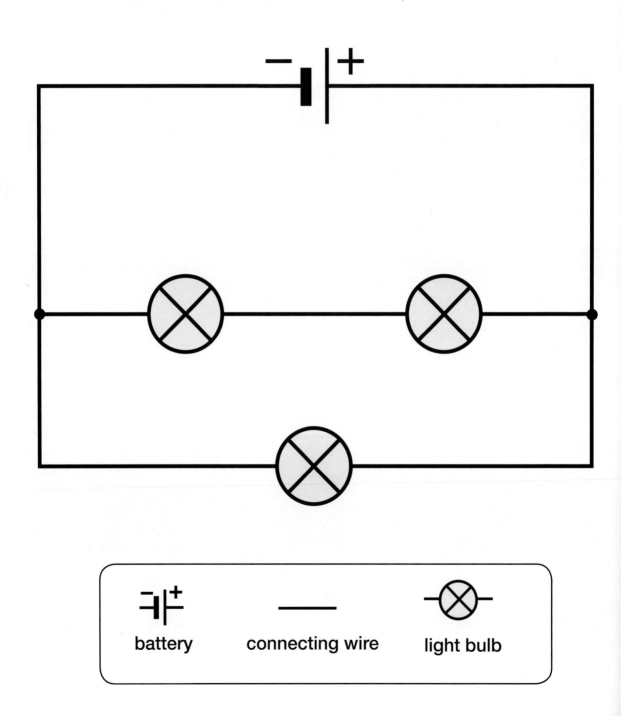

The electrical wiring in your house is an example of a parallel circuit. A source powers every light and appliance in the house. If one appliance is turned off, current still flows to the other devices. Many circuits are a combination of series and parallel circuits.

25

CHAPTER THREE

TYPES OF ELECTRIC CURRENT

There are two main types of electric current. They differ in the way the current travels on a circuit.

Direct current (DC) is the constant flow of electric charge in one direction. The amount of current may change, but it always flows in the same direction and takes the same path.

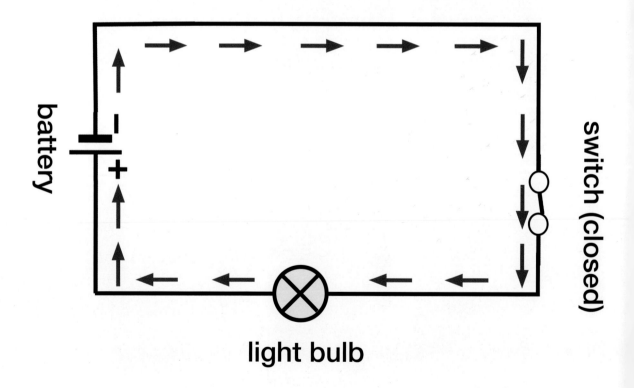

battery

switch (closed)

light bulb

A battery generates direct current. A battery has a positive (+) and a negative (-) end. When you connect the battery to a circuit, the electrons begin to flow in one direction. If you connect a lamp, you will see the lamp's light turn on as the current passes through it.

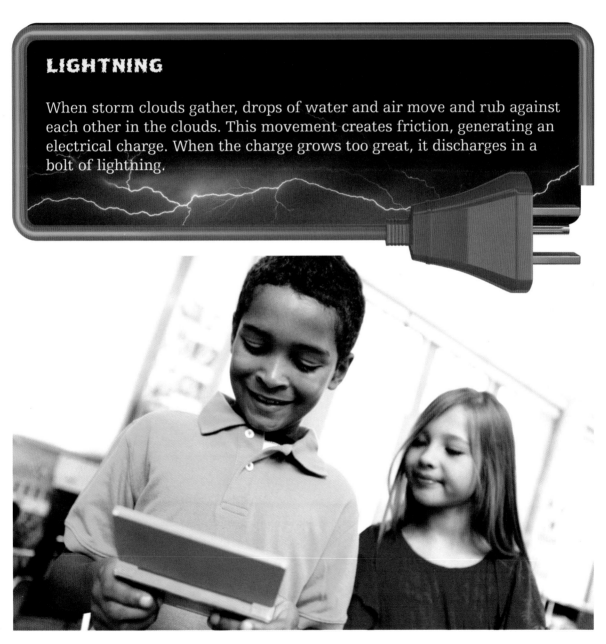

LIGHTNING

When storm clouds gather, drops of water and air move and rub against each other in the clouds. This movement creates friction, generating an electrical charge. When the charge grows too great, it discharges in a bolt of lightning.

Many people use direct current every day. Everything that uses batteries works on DC power. You use DC power to play handheld electronic games, light flashlights, and run portable radios.

Alternating current (AC) flows in one direction for a very short time. Then it reverses and flows in the opposite direction. Over and over, the current alternates its direction.

AC power is sent through power lines. The outlets in your home and anything that you plug into the wall, like a television, radio, or microwave, runs on AC power.

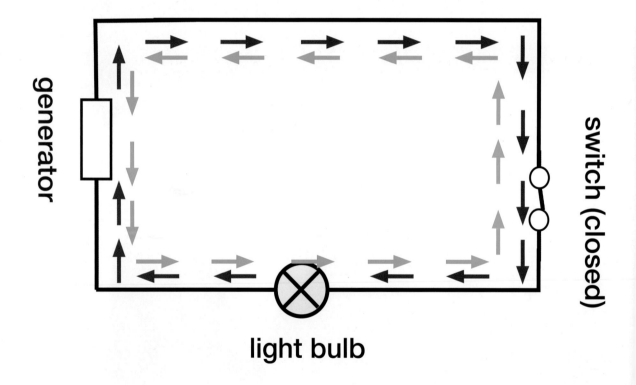

The cycle of switching directions is called frequency. Currents that switch directions or cycle more often have a higher frequency.

AC power has several advantages over DC power. It is cheaper to make in large quantities. AC power also holds its charge longer over long distances, and power plants can more easily adjust the amount of AC power being sent.

CHAPTER FOUR

GENERATING ELECTRIC CURRENT

Electric current travels a long distance before it reaches your house. The current's journey begins at a **power plant** where turbines and generators produce electricity.

A typical power plant **generator** uses an electromagnet to produce electricity. A series of wire coils form a stationary cylinder in which an electromagnetic shaft rotates. When the shaft moves, it creates a small electric current in the wire coils. The small currents then join together to form a large electric current.

Some generators have a rotating coil inside a fixed magnetic cylinder. This design is another way for the generator to produce electric current.

To run the generator, power plants use turbines, engines, or other devices. First, they use fuel to heat water in a boiler. When the water boils, it produces steam. The pressure of the steam moves the **turbine** and spins the electromagnetic shaft, producing the electric current.

A power plant uses a steam turbine to generate electricity.

MICHAEL FARADAY 1791-1867

In 1831, British scientist Michael Faraday found that moving an electric conductor through a magnetic field produced an electric current. It is called an induced current. In this way, the mechanical energy from moving the conductor is converted into electrical energy that flows in the wire. This principle is used to design today's modern electric generators.

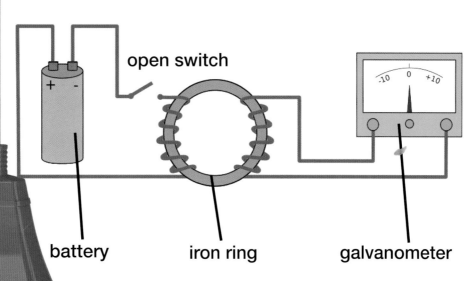

open switch

-10   0   +10

battery   iron ring   galvanometer

Faraday wrapped two insulated coils of wire around an iron ring. When he passed an electric current through one coil, an electric current was induced in the other coil.

Electricity can also be generated by wind power. A wind turbine looks like an enormous fan. Instead of using steam, the flow of air turns the blades to produce electricity.

The Sun can also generate electricity. Solar panels reflect sunlight to boil water. Its steam runs the generator.

Some communities near rivers or waterfalls use water to generate electricity. Hydroelectric energy uses flowing water to power electricity.

When electric current is generated, it has a lower voltage. To send electric current over a long distance, it is better to have a stronger **force** pushing it. A transformer changes the electric current from a low voltage to a high voltage.

This allows electric current to travel efficiently over long distances. The power plant is able to supply many homes and businesses.

Transmission lines carry the current to substations near the homes, businesses, and schools that will use the electricity. The substation converts the electric current back into a lower voltage before distributing it to the people who will use it.

CHAPTER FIVE

MEASURING ELECTRIC CURRENT

Have you ever wondered why the light bulb in your lamp may be marked 60 W? The W stands for **watt**, a unit of electrical power. The output from an electrical device is measured in watts. A light bulb with 75 W will burn brighter than a bulb with 30 W. Items with a very large output, such as a power plant, measure electricity in kilowatts. One kilowatt equals one thousand watts.

The watt was named after James Watt (1736–1819), a Scottish mechanical engineer and inventor. He improved the steam engine.

Voltage pushes an electric current along a wire in a circuit. A **volt** is the measure of this force. Voltage can come from a battery or power plant.

In the United States, the standard voltage delivered to homes is 120 volts. In Europe, the standard voltage is 240 volts. If you plug a lamp that is made to work on 240 volts into an outlet that delivers 120 volts, it will not work. On the other hand, if you plug a radio that uses 120 volts into an outlet that uses 240 volts, the higher voltage will damage the radio.

An electric current is measured in amperes. It is abbreviated as A or amps. An **ampere** measures how much electric current flows through a wire that is one millimeter ($\frac{3}{64}$ inches) in diameter in one second. If you imagine water pipes, a thick pipe allows more water to flow faster, while a skinny pipe allows less water through over the same time. In the same way, a thick cable made of several wires can carry more electric current than a single thin wire.

Some appliances use more electric current than others. For example, an electric oven requires more current than a lamp. Therefore, you need to know if the outlet the oven plugs into can deliver the correct amount of amps.

Electric currents power our world. The better we understand electricity, the better we understand the world we live in.

FUN FACT:

A tool called an ammeter measures the current in a circuit.

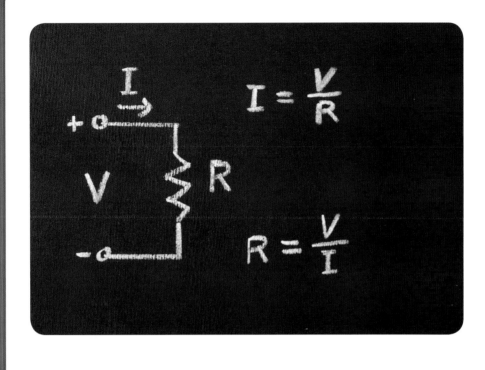

$$I = \frac{V}{R}$$

$$R = \frac{V}{I}$$

George Ohm (1789–1854) studied how materials conduct electricity. He showed that no material, even the best metal, was a perfect conductor. He proved that long wires have more **resistance** than short wires. He also observed that thin wires had more resistance than thick wires. More voltage was needed to push an electric current through thin wires.

With these observations, Ohm developed a formula to measure electrical resistance. Ohm's law says that the amount of current (I or amperes) that flows through a circuit equals the force (V or voltage) divided by the resistance (R or ohms).

GLOSSARY

alternating current (AWL-tuhr-nate-ing KUR-uhnt): current that changes directions many times every second

ampere (AM-pihr): a unit of electric current used to measure the rate at which electricity flows through a substance

atom (AT-uhm): the smallest part of an element

circuit (SUR-kit): the path along which electricity flows

conductor (kuhn-DUHK-tur): a material that allows electricity to flow easily

direct current (dye-REKT KUR-uhnt): current that flows in one direction all of the time

discharge (diss-CHARJ): the release of an electrical charge

electric current (i-lek-TRIK KUR-uhnt): the flow of electric charge, often carried by electrons

electron (i-LEK-tron): one of the very small, negatively charged particles that are part of an atom and are found outside an atom's nucleus

force (FORSS): a push or pull that gives energy to an object

generator (JEN-uh-ray-tur): a machine that creates electricity

insulators (IN-suh-late-turz): materials that stop the flow of electricity

load (LOHD): the power drained by a device or electrical circuit

parallel circuit (PA-ruh-lel SUR-kit): a circuit that connects a power source, load, and conductors in several loops

power plant (POU-ur PLANT): a place where generators make electricity for communities

resistance (ri-ZISS-tuhnss): a material that discourages or slows the flow of electricity

series circuit (SIHR-eez SUR-kit): a circuit that connects a power source, load, and conductors in a single loop

turbine (TUR-bine): a device that has a bladed wheel that is turned by the force of steam, gas, wind, or moving water

volt (VOHLT): a unit of for measuring the force of an electrical current

watt (WOT): a unit for measuring electrical power

INDEX

WEBSITES TO VISIT

kids.discovery.com/tell-me/curiosity-corner/science/
  how-do-electric-circuits-work

www.ducksters.com/science/physics/electric_current.php

www.brainpop.com/science/energy/currentelectricity/preview.weml

ABOUT THE AUTHOR

Carla Mooney has written many books for children and young adults. She lives in Pennsylvania with her husband and three children. She enjoys learning about science and appreciates all the gadgets electricity makes possible.

Meet The Author!
www.meetREMauthors.com

www.rourkeeducationalmedia.com

PHOTO CREDITS: title page, 3, 42 © gip311; page 4-5 © Rusian Dashinsky; page 6 © USBFCO; page 7, 9 © Stefan Chabluk; page 8, 10, 11, 12, 26, 28 © Jen Thomas; page 11, 13, 15, 21, 27, 33, 43, 45 © lucadp, Read Deal Photo; page 13, © pilq45, qn5iwhodk; page 14 © auremar; page 15 © Antonio Gravante; page 16 © ktsimage; page 17 © Designua; page 18 © Huntstock; page 19 © designua; page 20 © Elena Elisseeva; page 21 ironrodart; page 22, 24 © MilanB; page 23 © Viktor Gladkov; page 25 © Electrical Panel; page 27 © Recess funtime!, edstrom; page 29 © payphoto; page 30-31, 32, 37 © Arogant; page 33 © Dibner Library, james Bo Insogna, Eviatar Bach; page 34 © Grettchen; page 35 © adam smigiel; page 36 © 101dalmations; page 37 © Vaclar Volrab; page 39 Boris Sosnovyy; 40 © iodrakon; page 41 © fantasista; page 42 © SlipperPL; page 43 © PhotoSky; page 44 © auremar, Andrie Nekrassov; page 45 © ulrich knaupe, youri4u80

Edited by: Jill Sherman

Cover design by: Tara Raymo
Interior design by: Jen Thomas

Library of Congress PCN Data

It's Electric! Currents / Carla Mooney
(Let's Explore Science)
ISBN 978-1-62717-750-4 (hard cover)
ISBN 978-1-62717-872-3 (soft cover)
ISBN 978-1-62717-982-9 (e-Book)
Library of Congress Control Number: 2014935675

Also Available as: